ACROSS

THE

GREAT DIVIDE

A Memoir By

Christine A. Hillegass

While every precaution has been taken in the preparation of this book, the publisher assumes no responsibility for errors or omissions, or for damages resulting from the use of the information contained herein.

ACROSS THE GREAT DIVIDE: A MEMOIR

First edition. December 4, 2023.

Copyright © 2023 Christine A. Hillegass.

ISBN: 979-8223563266

Written by Christine A. Hillegass.

Table of Contents

For my husband Tom, my greatest champion

Prologue

I live in Montana, arguably one of the most beautiful places on earth. I've been here 25 years and I do love it. Even so, I never feel completely at home. The truth is I have had one foot in Montana and one foot on the East Coast of the U.S. my entire life. And that's a big straddle. While they are both "home" to me, I don't completely fit in in either place. While I'm in one place for any length of time I miss the other—the climate, the people, the place. This has certainly given me an appreciation for the culture in both places, but it has also left me feeling not completely "home" in either.

In Montana, there's nothing like the feeling you get from the open skies, the big vistas, and the mountains. When your line of sight extends unbroken for miles and miles, stretching to the horizon, it does something physical, it opens you up in some way, and helps you breathe. That's why it's called "Big Sky Country." Montana is wild, literally. We have grizzly bears, wolves, and wild, unpredictable weather that can be deadly. I think living here helps you reconnect to how small and vulnerable and frankly unimportant you are compared to the big, natural world.

But I miss the energy, richness, and stimulation of the art, music, dance, food, and erudition that is accessible in the urban Northeast. There is more urban history, more diversity, and more permission to be anyone you want to be. The extremes of social and creative expression give you breathing room in a different way. Maybe it's the difference between heart and mind.

Chapter One

I was born in Lancaster, Pennsylvania of mostly German and French Huguenot stock, with some Swiss and English thrown-in for good measure. I was born on July 13, 1952, but my life story of moving back and forth between the East and the West began even before I was born because I was conceived on the North Fork of the Shoshone River, just outside of the East entrance to Yellowstone National Park.

My mother and father, though both from Pennsylvania and married only about eight months, were living temporarily at the Elephant Head Ranch outside Cody, Wyoming. My dad was working in the fall of 1951 as a geologist with the Kennecott Copper Corp., doing exploratory geology along the Shoshone River, and thought it would be more fun to live on a ranch instead of in town in an apartment. I'm not sure if my mom thought this was so fun, but she went along with it. After a number of months there, they went back to Pennsylvania where I was born. But then, when I was only three months old, my dad got a position with the Anaconda Copper Company and they moved back West to Butte, Montana.

Let me tell you, Butte in 1952 was a world away from Southeastern Pennsylvania. Although it had at one time been the biggest city between Chicago and San Francisco, Butte was basically one big mining town, with over 60 mining head frames (the black metal structures above underground mine shafts) spread out across the whole town. Because of the influx of miners from all over the world (China, Wales, Ireland, Finland, Austria, Italy, Serbia, etc.), Butte earned a wild reputation with saloons, a red light district called Venus Alley, and brothels still operating even into the 1980s. Eventually the city's growth began to decline due to the increasing costs of copper mining and low copper prices. At the time my parents lived there the population had dropped from roughly

100,000 to about 30,000. There was one college, though not a liberal arts school, called the Butte School of Mines. Otherwise, there were no "high culture" amenities like you'd find in big cities, and they had a heck of a lot of snow for a good seven or eight months out of the year.

We lived in Butte for about a year and a half, but in the spring of 1954 my father got laid off from Anaconda. Because my mother was again pregnant, we moved back to Pennsylvania, where my sister Elizabeth Bertolet (Bebe) was born in June. At first we lived with my mother's parents in Lancaster.

My mother, Ann Christine Wolf Hillegass, (b: 5/6/31), was born and raised in Lancaster. She was the only child of her parents, Anna Harmes Wolf and Clarence A. Wolf. My grandmother was a college-educated school teacher and my grandfather worked for the Armstrong Cork Company, eventually working his way up into the engineering department. Although surrounded by Pennsylvania Dutch farm country, Lancaster in the 1930s and 1940s was a city of about 61,000 people. Franklin and Marshall College made it a college town, with a fair number of cultural attributes. For example, Lancaster had department stores, a local symphony, and a country club. Furthermore, Philadelphia was only an hour and a half away by train.

My mother had been a piano protégé as a child. The story goes that at age 5 or 6 she would go, by herself, down the street to the First Presbyterian Church so she could play the organ. From age 16, she took the train to Philadelphia every week for classes at the Conservatory of Music (now called the University of the Arts), and began teaching piano at about the same time. By 19, she was teaching about 40 students. But it was the 1950s when women's careers were not valued. So my mother (surprisingly, since her own mother was college educated and had a career) gave up graduating from the Philadelphia Conservatory to marry my father.

The New Jersey Seashore was only about three hours away from Lancaster and my mother and her family would go there every summer. Along the Atlantic Coast, from New York City to Philadelphia to Wilmington, Delaware, the Jersey Shore had since the mid-1800s been THE destination in the summer, when the first shore resorts were built for the rich and affluent. But now, particularly after World War II, the average white man could afford to go. (Unfortunately, most Black people were still the servants and maids, etc., and didn't have the economic or social privileges that whites had.) I think about how my mother would have just turned 15 in the summer of 1946, 16 in '47, and 17 in '48, when the country was high from having won the War, the vets were back, and all the boys who'd have been too young to serve were coming of age. Her family would have been down in Ocean City, Wildwood, and Cape May, when money for building more hotels and motels, amusement rides for the boardwalks, eateries, and dancehalls, was pouring into the Shore towns. Cars were getting faster, girls were being allowed more freedoms, and it was the era of swing bands and the Lindy Hop. The seashore, with its cool sea breezes and ocean, was the place to escape the oppressive heat of the cities and inland communities, since most people couldn't afford air conditioning yet, and people hadn't yet been warned about skin cancer, so sun worshipping was more than fashionable. Although I didn't inherit any family photographs of that time, I know my mother loved the Jersey Seashore.

My father, Michael Hillegass (b: 2/29/28), was also an only child, and was raised in Upper Montgomery County, about 48 miles northwest of Philadelphia. In the 1930s and '40s, this was very rural Pennsylvania Dutch country. His mother was a high school-educated, stay-at-home mom and his father was an attorney. Although he had been taken to Philadelphia and New York City as a youngster, my dad's childhood was unlike my mother's urban upbringing. In addition to living in a rural farming community, my grandparents also spent quite a bit of time "roughing it" in the North Maine woods in the summers, taking my dad and staying in a rustic lake camp.

One of the characters from that time was Levi Dow. Levi was the sole game warden and police presence for the whole district and he owned the camp where my grandparents stayed. He was 6'4" and was built like a "powerhouse." As one of the stories goes, one time some guests arrived in a big Cadillac from Boston. The next morning, when the lady came out of her cabin in her bathrobe and slippers, with her towel over her arm and a cake of soap in her hand, she asked Levi, "Pahdon me, where is the bahth?" Apparently, Levi took the soap and heaved it out into the lake, saying, "Lady, there's a whole g-d lake." Levi didn't 'cotton' much to those fussy, city-types.

At any rate, when we returned to Pennsylvania from Butte in 1954, my father re-evaluated his geology career. Eventually he decided to follow in his father's footsteps and applied to go to law school. From Lancaster we moved to suburban Philadelphia while he went to the University of Pennsylvania. After he graduated and passed the Pennsylvania Bar Exam in 1958 (I was 6 and my sister 4), we moved out to rural Montgomery County, where his parents still lived and where he subsequently opened a law practice. Until I was in eighth grade we lived out in the country outside of the town where my grandparents lived and where my dad's office was. The population of the township back then was approximately 9,000. Across the road from our house was a cornfield, next to us was a cow pasture, and behind us was a big hill, at the bottom of which was a creek, and across the creek were woods. I wasn't particularly crazy about the cornfield or the smelly cow pasture, but I did love playing on the hill and in the creek and the woods. My grandparents also by this time owned a camp on a lake in Maine so we often vacationed up there. While there I was introduced for the first time to mountains. Although relatively small, at 5,269 feet Mount Katahdin is one of the tallest mountains in the Northeast and is near a stretch of the

Appalachian Trail known as The Hundred-Mile Wilderness. All through my growing up years we were also taken to the Jersey Shore by both sets of grandparents.

As I said, Upper Montgomery County was rural Pennsylvania Dutch country. To clarify, Pennsylvania Dutch is not the same thing as Amish. Amish and Mennonite are religions, and their people began emigrating because of persecution in Europe. For the most part those groups settled in Lancaster, Berks, Lebanon, and Chester counties, not in Montgomery County, which is further north and east. But Pennsylvania Dutch is a language and a culture that was brought to the Southeastern part of Pennsylvania in the early to late 1700s, when many Protestant Alsatian and Germanic peoples also came, bringing their food and language with them, and were thus labeled Pennsylvania German or Pennsylvania Deutsch. When I was growing up in the 1950s and early 1960s, my grandfather still spoke Pennsylvania Dutch, and he had farming clients in his law practice whom he could only communicate with in this way. In many ways, this sub-culture reminds me of the Cajun culture in Louisiana with its distinct food and language, though it has not been romanticized or preserved as that culture has been—perhaps because their music has brought them more fame and media attention.

Over the years I've been asked numerous times if I'm Amish. No, my family background is Protestant. However, my dad's mother's parents were both raised Mennonite in Lancaster County. They married and left the faith back at the turn of the last century and raised their family in the city of Lancaster. But because of this background, my grandmother did have Mennonite farm cousins who lived "out in the County," as they say. Subsequently, from both of my grandmothers I learned many of the traditional Pennsylvania Dutch recipes like pork and sauerkraut, knepp dumplings, and shoofly pie.

When I was 13, my dad got a job with the Philadelphia Defenders Association (Philadelphia's version of Legal Aid) and we moved to the city. This move turned out to give me one of the most impactful experiences of my life. The rural community where we had lived was insular and prone to typical small-town behavior: gossip and shunning people who were different. I had been a shy kid without many friends, definitely not in the popular group. In seventh or eighth grade when a new girl moved into town and started school, on the first day of class no other kids spoke to her or made her feel welcome, instead staring at her like she was a freak or something. I remember feeling embarrassed and badly for her, though I have to admit that because of my own shyness and lack of confidence, I did nothing to help her. Well, when we moved into West Philadelphia, I got to be the new kid.

On my first day of school at the Henry C. Lea Elementary & Junior High School, which was about 80% black and 20% white, the homeroom teacher introduced me to the class. I'll never forget this as long as I live—and even now as I write this it brings tears to my eyes. Nearly every one of those kids jumped up out of their seats and circled my desk, calling out their names and sticking their hands out to shake mine. I didn't have time to be scared because they were all smiling and saying welcoming things. Then across the room I saw what looked like the "cool" kids, sort of standing apart. One boy and one girl were Black, the other two were white. I thought they looked like beatniks (it was 1966). At some point the Black girl came over to me and asked if I would like them to walk me home, and said she and her "group" went to a local hangout after school for sodas if I'd like to come with them. Of course I said yes, and from that moment on Brenda became one of my best friends.

In all of my eight grades of schooling no one had ever made me feel the way these kids made me feel. I know that this contributed to my beginning to come out of my shell and develop more self-confidence. More than anything, though, it led to my belief that Black people are kinder than white people. Though I know now that generalizations like that aren't true, it has left me with lifelong affection and sympathy for Black people.

Thus I spent my high school years living in West Philadelphia, which was a more diverse, liberal, sophisticated culture. I remember going back to the high school in Montgomery County for a visit during ninth grade, wearing a Mondrian dress and fishnet stockings, and feeling as though I was literally visiting from Mars. My family had friends who were Black and Jewish and Italian and Quaker and Unitarian. It was the late-1960s and my sister and I took subways all over the city and went to anti-war and civil-rights marches and folk and rock concerts. We hung out after school and in the summer down at Rittenhouse Square, where African dancers performed and hippies played guitars and bongos. We also went to the Israeli folk dances that were held at the Philadelphia Museum of Art on summer nights.

From there I went to Bard College in upstate New York, on the Hudson River, two hours north of New York City. Thus, I was back living in the country again. The Hudson Valley is known for its lush, green rolling hills. Across the river from the campus we could see the Catskill Mountains. Sometimes on weekends my friends and I would go over to explore the other side of the river. I loved driving the winding mountain roads, with steep rocky drop-offs and roaring waterfalls, to the quaint mountain and ski towns of the Catskill region.

During the summer between my sophomore and junior year, my grandparents decided to take my family to a dude ranch in Montana. It was 1973, nearly 20 years since my folks and I had been back. We spent two weeks at the 320 Ranch on the Gallatin River, south of the town of Bozeman. At that time Patty and Jimmy Goodrich owned the Ranch. This was in the days when Chet Huntley had purchased the land up at what would become the Big Sky Resort; though building had begun, the valley along the Gallatin was still pristine undeveloped ranch land. We rode horses every day, saw black bears, smelled sagebrush, breathed in the incredible mountain vistas, and, naturally, my sister and I both had romances with the cowboys. I absolutely fell in love with Montana. More significantly, this vacation led to my parents making a huge decision and changing the trajectory of my life.

When we got home to Philadelphia in late August, it was one of those days in the 1970s when the combination of heat, humidity, and air pollution turned the sky a horrid yellowish color. I'll never forget the day we got off the airplane, because the contrast with the arid, clear, 80-degree days in Montana was absolutely shocking. My father almost turned around and went back into the airport.

Although my sister and I returned to our respective colleges, I was not completely surprised when my parents called less than two months later and said they were putting our house on the market and moving to Montana (just like the Frank Zappa song). The timing made sense because my dad had not been happy in his job for some time and there were changes happening in our Powelton Village neighborhood that were making it an increasingly unpleasant place to live. Specifically, in the past year a weird cult had moved into a house just one block down the street from us. I say weird because they didn't seem to have any particular philosophy or plan, but called themselves MOVE, and were led by some guy named John Africa. They appeared to be a commune of some kind, with numerous women and lots of babies, and the only belief they seemed to have was that it was their right to throw their garbage (including dirty diapers) right into their front yard. The city hadn't done anything about the situation, so my fed-up mother took herself down the street to confront them. My father was apoplectic, as he was sure she'd get her head blown off. I wish I had a recording of this. Here's my tiny, 4'11" mother standing at their gate, demanding that they clean up their house before they bring rats and worse into the neighborhood.

Not surprisingly, her tirade didn't yield any results, so, the following May, 1974, incredibly, my parents left Philadelphia and moved to Montana. An interesting addendum to this story is that after the city finally forced MOVE out of that house, the cult proceeded to relocate to another in West Philly. Sometime after we had moved away, a fiasco erupted that gained national attention when the mayor bombed their house and burnt down the whole block on which they were living.

I joined my parents in Montana again that summer for a few weeks. First we stayed at the 320 Ranch for another week, and then we spent some time touring around Park County, the next county over, where they were looking to buy property. I still couldn't get over the dry, clear air and the beauty of the place. How do you describe Montana to those who have never seen it? First, there are many places where you can see across miles and miles of green and tawny-colored land, almost devoid of people. Here and there, a few houses, ranches, and cows and horses dot the landscape. Then there are small hills, bluffs, and ridges carved by glaciers that look covered in green and fawn-colored velvet. Next, huge, craggy mountains that really are purple stretch upwards from the valley floor to 10,000 feet, and are mostly snow-capped until late summer. On the valley floors meander tree-lined creeks and rivers. Lastly, practically anywhere you are you can see the horizon and giant whipped-cream clouds boiling upwards to 30,000 feet or more. It's all so big and spacious, it feels almost indescribable.

One of the things we did that summer was go on a three-day pack trip up into the mountains at the edge of Yellowstone Park. We rode our horses all day into the wilderness and then camped at a lake at the foot of Electric Peak. For three days we saw no one other than a Ranger who came into our camp one night while we were sitting around the campfire jawing. The weather and scenery were beautiful. Reaching about 80 degrees in the daytime, when we woke up in our sleeping bags in the morning we could see our breath. While we were there, we ate fish from the lake and rode up to the top of Electric Peak, which rises to 10,969 feet. On top we had a complete 360-degree unobstructed view of the surrounding country. I remember being amazed that when we looked over the edge back down to our campsite, the lake was just this little bitty thing down at the bottom.

I hated to leave and go back East, but I had to go back to return for my last year of school. The first couple of years I had double majored in English literature and psychology. My maternal grandmother had been an English teacher and had always encouraged my writing. Because I enjoyed and excelled at writing papers in my psychology classes, I dropped the other major and concentrated on psych.

Bard College was a pretty idyllic place. In addition to a serious academic curriculum, we had strong art, music, drama, and dance departments, which contributed a lot of entertainment to campus life. We had outdoor, Woodstock-like music concerts, one could hike through the woods to the "Deserted Village" where a former student was rumored to be living while building a cement boat, and in early September and late May one might even go skinny dipping in the waterfall on the Sawkill River, which ran by the campus. And I mustn't forget the urban myth that Bob Dylan had hung out at Bard at one time, based on our certainty that the line "the vandals stole the handle" from his "Subterranean Homesick Blues" was a reference to the old fashioned water pump in nearby Annandale. Because I loved being there and because my boyfriend, John Duke Kisch, still had one more year to go, I got a job in the area and stayed for another year after I graduated. I suppose one of the reasons I loved Bard so much was because in two hours you could be in NYC and in less than two hours you could be across the Hudson up in the Catskill Mountains.

In 1976, after John graduated, we moved to Manhattan and took over his family's rent-controlled apartment while he was getting a start as a photographer in the fashion industry. I lived in New York for four years, during which I got my master's degree in forensic psychology and started working in the mental health field. I had been entertaining the idea of going to law school and following in my father's and grandfather's footsteps, but wasn't sure if I wanted to pursue a career in psychology instead, so I thought getting this degree might help me decide.

New York was like Philadelphia on steroids. I could get any kind of food delivered to my apartment door at practically any time of night, in one given trip through the subways I might hear languages from all over the world being spoken, and I could go from shopping in Chinatown or at Bloomingdales during the day to either a jazz club or the Metropolitan Opera that night. We did go out to clubs because John knew people in the music business, but they weren't all high-class spots. For example, one of our haunts was called the Bells of Hell. One of my favorite memories was our first Thanksgiving. Our apartment was on 77th Street between Columbus Avenue and Central Park West. On Thanksgiving morning, while we were working on the first turkey either of us had ever made, they were blowing up the huge Macy's Day Parade balloons right outside our windows!

Unfortunately, though I did feel that John was the love of my life, it became apparent that we weren't working and in the end we broke up. As much as we loved one another, we wanted different things and probably would have made each other miserable. Anyway, I eventually got priced out of the city. Even though I was now working as a young professional psychologist, I couldn't afford anything in Manhattan but windowless, basement studio apartments, and I didn't want to move to Brooklyn, which wasn't as fashionable then as it has since become.

During these years I continued to visit my parents in Livingston, Montana, where they had decided to settle. Livingston (approximate 1980 population: 7,000) is in the Southwest corner of the state, on the

Yellowstone River, and about an hour north of the Gardiner entrance to Yellowstone Park. It is the county seat for Park County (at that time pop.15,000), is surrounded by approximately 2,500 square miles of ranch land and mountains, and is the only major town in the county. Not only a historical entrance to the National Park, Livingston was also known for its award-winning trout fishing. Another one of Livingston's claims to fame was that its train depot in the center of town was designed by the same architecture firm that designed Grand Central Station in NYC.

Visiting my parents there, I thought I was living the wild life alright; there I was in my mid-20s, living in NYC and vacationing in the "Wild West." This is a key to my divided loyalties that still persist. I couldn't get over the fact that there was even a western wear shop right in the center of town where you could get a pair of cowboy boots and a hat. On one of my trips my folks took me down to Cody, Wyoming, named after Buffalo Bill Cody. We went to a rodeo, and to the Buffalo Bill Art Museum, of course we had to go out to see the Elephant Head Ranch where they had lived, and we stayed at the historic Irma Hotel, which Buffalo Bill named after one of his daughters. While there, I bought a stuffed Jackalope head, which I of course took back to New York with me.

While in Livingston, my folks introduced me to some people my age, and after a day of trail riding, or hiking up to the top of a mountain, or floating the Yellowstone, or taking a road trip down to Jackson Hole, my friends would take me out to the bars in town. The Long Branch Saloon actually had old-time swinging saloon doors, and next door was The Wrangler. So as to not compete with one another, they would switch off which nights they had live music. One specialized more in country-western, and the other in rock'n'roll. Then after closing time, we'd spill across the street to Martin's Café, an old-style diner that was open 24 hours a day, for breakfast of course. One of the things I learned from the cowboys who came in from the ranches on Friday and Saturday nights was never to take a cowboy's hat and sassily put it on your head, because it means you're going home with him!

Livingston was also popular with the Hollywood set in those days. Peter Fonda and Jeff Bridges both had places outside of town in Paradise Valley. Jimmy Buffet even wrote a song about it called, "Livingston Saturday Night," which was released on a 45 RPM that I took with me back East and still have today.

So I had to move out of Manhattan. Because for as long as I could remember I had never lived in the suburbs—which to me just seemed like pablum (forgive me, I was only 27)—I looked into moving to the northern Jersey Shore. Having always gone as a kid to the southern Jersey Shore, I had never been there before, but a couple of my work friends lived there and convinced me to check it out. So on one excursion to look at a house share situation in Long Branch, New Jersey, I discovered that there was, nearby, an actual bar called, yes, The Long Branch Saloon. To me that was a sure sign that I had found the right place. Not to mention the fact that I could share a three-story house less than a block from the beach for about a third of the cost of a studio in New York. Another good thing about the northern Jersey Shore was that it was within commuter distance of NYC, so I still had easy access to the city either by train or car. I timed it once: driving I could get from my house in Long Branch to Greenwich Village and be parked in one hour and ten minutes.

I then lived in Monmouth County, New Jersey, for 18 years. Over the years I moved to several different places, but I loved living at the Shore. Though I never learned to surfboard, I was a pretty serious body surfer, and from mid-May to mid-September I half lived at the beach. The trick was to get all my weekly chores done by noon on Saturday so I could spend the rest of the weekend down on the beach. Because it was so flat I also became an avid bicycle rider, sometimes riding 20 miles or more. And of course, because of living there, I became a Bruce Springsteen fan. Before that I had mostly been into jazz and old-time country-western, western swing, bluegrass, and country/folk rock, and of course the classical music I had heard at home. I certainly also followed the major rock'n'roll artists; in fact by the time I was in my early 30s I considered myself a bit of an amateur musicologist. But I could hardly live in the radius of Asbury Park and not become a Springsteen fan. Bruce apparently even used to play on the beach right in front of that first house I rented on Atlantic Avenue, though unfortunately it was before I lived there. Another strange coincidental fact was that just a block down from there was a house that was rumoured to have been built and used by Buffalo Bill Cody for his summer headquarters when performing in the New York metropolitan area.

Because the house I lived in was practically on the beach, within a couple of months I made friends with some locals through whom I met Corny (short for Cornelius). Corny was a blonde, tanned, hippie artist who lived nearby in an old lighthouse building. He was a lot of fun, and liked to laugh. I had decided that one characteristic in a guy that was really important to me was having a good sense of humor—and he did. Sleeping up on the top floor of his lighthouse with 360-degree windows, just feet from the ocean, also made our courting very romantic, and he was a sweet guy. Another cute detail was that he was friends with one of Springsteen's ex-girlfriends and she had given him some of the clothes Springsteen had left at her place. When we were first going out, he was wearing Bruce's purple swim briefs! Anyway, I did a really good job of ignoring some serious warning signs while being impressed by his positive characteristics. I grew to love him and after a couple of years, we got married.

Corny and I honeymooned in Livingston. We stayed in my parents' house, spent time with my friends, got invited to parties on ranches, went to Chico Hot Springs and wildlife watching in Yellowstone, and borrowed a car from one of my friends and spent four days up in Glacier National Park.

At this point my parents had moved back to Pennsylvania, although they hadn't sold their house yet. This was now 1983. Their decision to move back East was a complicated one. My dad loved living in Montana, but my mother—having always been more of a "city girl"—had never been as happy being out west. She wasn't into hiking, riding, or floating the Yellowstone. Her idea of hiking was walking in and out of stores, restaurants, and concerts. By 1982 she went back to Pennsylvania for what they thought was going to be a short-term visit to take care of her ailing, elderly mother, but it turned into almost a year. Then there was the fact that Livingston entered an economic downturn. One of Livingston's two major industries was the Northern Pacific Railroad (the other being tourism), but they decided to pull out the majority of their train repair yard, cutting something like 600 jobs in town. This immediately reduced my father's law practice and left him struggling to find work. One thing led to another and they decided to put the Livingston house on the market and permanently move back to Pennsylvania.

I was disappointed that my folks decided to sell their house instead of keeping it for us for vacationing. And, unfortunately, after our honeymoon, I could not get Corny interested in returning to Montana and thus I did not go back for 14 years. This was only one of the bones of contention that wrecked our marriage. There were serious personality problems involving alcohol and anger that I hadn't wanted to see, and it took me a long time, and lots of therapy and Al-Anon, to face that I couldn't fix him. During these years I had decided to go back to school and in 1993 got my doctorate in clinical psychology. The further I went in my education, the less I could ignore the painful reality of our situation, which ultimately led me to the sad conclusion that I had to leave Corny.

It was sometime during these years when I was in my 40s that it dawned on me that I had actually realized two childhood dreams. I remembered that as an older teenager while visiting the seashore, I had not wanted to go home at the end of one vacation and was jealous of those who lived there year-round. And here I was for years basically living within a half mile of the beach! Then I realized that when I was a pre-teen living in the country in Pennsylvania I had wished that one day I could live in NYC like the fashion models in my *Teen* and *Seventeen* magazines. Not only had I lived in Manhattan, but with a fashion photographer! It was so uncanny to realize that though I was not aware of living my life consciously aiming at these goals, I had apparently subliminally achieved them anyway!

Chapter Two

Here's where I need to go back and explain how I know that my love affair with Montana was influenced by my dad's romance with the West, which didn't start when he first worked out there in 1951, but went back to his childhood. First of all, he grew up reading things like *Smoky*, and other Will James books. He also grew up hearing tales his parents told about their trips out West in the 1920s. His mother's eldest brother, J. Wilmer Hershey, who was an architect, had moved to California to take advantage of the development going on there after World War I. He actually designed many of the early buildings in San Clemente. Unfortunately, while there he became ill with Addison's disease and my grandmother, Ruth Shaub Hershey, took a cross-country train trip out to Los Angeles to help. In the 1920s passenger flights from the East Coast to California didn't exist yet, so she had to go by train. Sadly, after he died, she helped bring his wife, Sarah, and their two boys back to Pennsylvania. Though a tragic event in my grandmother's life to be sure, she nevertheless always portrayed this trip as an exciting adventure for a young woman from the East.

My grandfather, J. B. "Jack" Hillegass, had driven out to California about this same time. While a student at Franklin & Marshall College, in Lancaster—where my grandmother Ruth was coincidentally raised—he had befriended another one of my grandmother's brothers (she had five). In fact, J.B. and Ivan were fraternity brothers at Franklin & Marshall. The Hershey household was known for often having guests, so my grandfather had been out to the family home where he of course had met my grandmother. My grandfather graduated from F&M in 1920 and though he went on to Harvard Law School, he remained friends with Ivan. Sometime after he graduated from Harvard they decided to drive cross-country to California. My father of course had heard the tales of this trip when he was growing up. Not only had the interstate highway system not been built, but apparently west of the Mississippi many of the roads in the early 1920s were still dirt. I can just picture Jack and Ivan in my granddad's Willis-Knight Convertible – you know, the kind with the accordion convertible canvas top – bumping along across the vast open West. One of the adventures they related happened in a town in Texas where they had stopped for gas. They asked the fellow there where they could get something to eat and a rancher who had overheard them invited them out to his place and fed them. He probably had never seen anybody from outside the county much less from back East. Anyway, he ended up giving my granddad a great big sombrero at least two feet across, with black fringe and pompoms hanging all around the edge. I still remember seeing that up in my grandparents' attic when I was a kid.

Apparently while Granddad and Great-Uncle Ivan were in Los Angeles, the romance between Ruth and Jack blossomed, and eventually led to them getting married after they both returned to Pennsylvania. They spent a short time as young marrieds living in Philadelphia, but after my father was born they moved to the small town of Pennsburg, which was my grandfather's family home. As I've said, when my father was growing up this was still a very rural Pennsylvania Dutch farming community.

When my dad was 12 his parents took him on his first trip out West, in 1940. They flew out to Burbank, California, where they picked up a car, and then drove north to San Francisco, then to Salt Lake, and then on to Evergreen, Colorado, for a national Sigma Pi fraternity convention. This is where my dad got his first experience in western horseback riding, trail riding with a wrangler up in the mountains of the Colorado Rockies. He told me stories about how he'd go loping off into the distance, much to the chagrin of the wrangler. One time he came to a fork in the road and yelled back, "Which way?" and the wrangler yelled to him, "The other way." My dad said he stood there awhile trying to figure out what that meant. By then they had all pulled up to him, at which point the wrangler said, "Well now you can get in the back of the line." And THAT was my dad.

Sometime around this period he had managed to costume himself in a complete cowboyin' outfit the likes of which, I'm sure anyone would have been proud.

In 1948, while my dad was in college, his parents had a friend who mentioned that he was looking for someone to take a summer job as a cook's aid/dishwasher out at a dude ranch in Montana. This friend was going to drive West in his Woody station wagon, taking the cook and three college guys who were going to be wranglers. My dad jumped at the chance. Six guys drove all the way out to Montana with all of their gear, and with two standard poodles, no less. The ranch turned out to be the B-Bar-K Ranch on the Gallatin River, owned by the Butler-Kilbourne family.

This ranch was sold in the 1970s to Chet Huntley, to be part of Big Sky, and is today called Lone Mountain Guest Ranch. My dad got to ride horses every day, up into the Spanish Peaks of the Gallatins, even taking long day trips. He has told me about how attached he got to that horse named Big Red.

One time when they were out late and coming back on the trail, he couldn't see a thing in front of him but, Big Red was trotting right along rapidly. Suddenly the horse stopped short and wouldn't budge. Dad kicked him, argued with him, but he could not get him to move. At that point he put his hand out in front of his face and at arm's length found a fixed tree branch right across the trail that would have knocked him clear out of the saddle. He bent low, put his cheek against the horse's neck, and Big Red immediately, without even being prodded, walked on.

Years later, when we as a family stayed on the 320 Ranch in the Gallatin, my Dad and Jimmy Goodrich recognized one another immediately when we walked in the door of the main lodge. Jimmy had been the head wrangler at the B-Bar-K and now owned his own ranch!

My dad, like his dad, also attended Franklin & Marshall College, and just like my grandparents' story, he met and fell in love with a Lancaster girl, my mother. Even though she was still in high school she had attended parties at his fraternity where they met. But before they got married, when my dad was 22, he took another trip out West. In the summer of 1950, when he graduated, he took a four-month, cross-country trip with one of his fraternity brothers. They drove the used Ford police car my dad had bought in '49, which had a hole in the roof where the police strobe light had been. They carried tents and bedrolls and tools, an ax, and two extra tires and even a gas can, which they roped onto the top. From Lancaster there was a four-lane turnpike, but for most of the rest of the way they drove on two-lane roads. They went through Kentucky and Missouri, and bathed in the Cimarron River in Oklahoma. He told a funny story about how when they came out of the river, they were all red. At first they thought it was sunburn and didn't discover until they eventually got to a motel that the red dirt washed off!

They picked up Route 66 in Oklahoma, and mostly followed that all the way to Los Angeles, although they did a fair amount of zig-zagging around in the Southwest.

They decided to stop in Albuquerque for a month to make some money. They stayed with friends of my grandparents who got them jobs at the Shriners Fez Club, and in their free time they went horseback riding and chased jackrabbits. From there they went north up to Santa Fe where they stopped at a diner. They talked with the owner, who strangely had a Brooklyn accent. He regaled them with stories of having been in the Pacific Ocean Theater and about being discharged in San Francisco and deciding to drive across America. He couldn't believe how big and beautiful and different the country was from Brooklyn, and decided that he just wasn't going any farther and bought the diner and that was that! This is one of those stories you will hear over and over again about why some people decide to settle down where they do in the West.

Another one of my dad's stories involved their deciding to explore and go "off–road." They had heard about a trading post on the Navajo reservation and started west on a dirt road that was not on any map. It wound around, becoming smaller and rougher until it was nothing more than a bare track that went higher and higher on a ridge, to the point that they couldn't even see the track any longer. My dad had to get out and help guide his buddy around big rocks, ruts, and holes, until suddenly they came to a big drop-off. Down at the bottom they could see what was called Mexican Hat, a tiny community named for the nearby sombrero-shaped rock formation. This area is known as the Four Corners area, where Utah, Colorado, New Mexico, and Arizona meet. In order to get down from there they had to negotiate steep switchbacks down the cliff face to the bottom. This hair-raising story is typical of my dad, often wanting to go his "own way." I wonder today how his car ever survived this trip!

They decided to drive through the Mojave Desert at night to avoid the heat. Even then it was in the 90s. Dad remembers seeing people carrying canvas bags of water on the outside of their vehicles, and also a newfangled air-conditioner that hung outside of the passenger car window. Often known as Firestone Thermidors, these were basically swamp coolers that directed the cool air into the interior of the car. Another anecdote he loved to tell was how to make a jam sandwich in a moving car: you put a piece of bread on each knee, then you put the bread away, and then put peanut butter on one piece, and jelly on the other, and then you "jam" your knees together!

Some years before, my dad's Aunt Sarah had moved back to California and was living in El Monte, a town in the Los Angeles suburbs. They headed to her house and then of course had to see the Pacific Ocean, where apparently my dad's buddy wanted to relieve himself "for old times' sake," and where my dad remembers seeing the new modern freeways.

From there they headed up through Yosemite National Park and then on to Salt Lake, where they conveniently planned to meet up with my grandparents who were going to be there for another Sigma Pi convocation meeting. By this time my dad and his buddy had basically run out of money and only made it to Salt Lake by coasting into gas stations, pulling up to the pump, and sneaking a couple drips out of the pump nozzle. Naturally, my grandfather helped out so they didn't have to ditch the car and hitchhike back to Pennsylvania.

I had heard these stories throughout my growing up years. Plus, my parents and my paternal grandmother had saved photographs of our early life, so I grew up seeing photos that had been taken of my parents and me in Butte, and of vacations that we took out to Cannon Beach, Oregon, and through Glacier Park to the Prince of Wales Hotel in Canada. However, back then that seemed very foreign to me, like looking at pictures of someone else's life. After my sister was born we never returned to Montana through all of my childhood so I didn't identify myself with anything other than being an Easterner. But I loved when my father regaled us with his stories, which to me seemed like such romantic adventures. I too was captured by the romance of the West, which I was exposed to not through books, as my dad had been, but through the western television shows that dominated the airwaves in the 1950s and early 1960s: "My Friend Flicka," "Sky King," "Roy Rogers," "Fury," "The Virginian," "Bonanza," "Annie Oakley." It didn't matter whether it was Saturday afternoon or weekday evenings, I wanted to watch them, I wanted to be <u>in</u> them, I wanted to BE them.

When I was little, my father also had a guitar. He told me how he had fallen in love with old-time cowboy/folk music and had started strumming someone's guitar that summer he was out at the B-Bar-K. Apparently when he came back to Pennsylvania afterwards, he discovered that his grandfather Hillegass had an old guitar up in the attic with gut strings on it and had subsequently taught himself how to play. He would sing things like Burl Ives' "Big Rock Candy Mountain," or cowboy tunes like "Cool Clear Water." He'd don his "old" cowboy hat from his days in Montana (it might only have been 10 years earlier, but to me, at age 11, it was from a different world than the one I was living in) and play his guitar and sing cowboy music, and I would be transported to the "ole campfire," even while sitting right in our house in Pennsylvania. It seemed to my 11-year-old self that cowgirls and cowboys had as many adventures as the models I read about in my *Teen* magazines. I felt my small-town, rural life was boring.

On the other hand, I was also raised in a household where classical music was played regularly, either on the stereo or by my mother. I took piano and ballet lessons, was taken to Philadelphia to go shopping, and to see the ballet and the Philadelphia Orchestra. All through my youth my mother continued to teach piano, and never stopped playing her grand piano. That Chickering piano was always a fixture in our home, even going to and from Montana with them. My mother insisted that my sister and I learn how to play, though I wasn't happy about it. Eventually she allowed me to take ballet lessons instead. But I did love listening to her play. In fact, I idolized her playing and never felt I could begin to compete with her. My favorite memory is dancing in our living room as a child to her playing the de Falla "Ritual Fire Dance." I imagined myself in a fabulous costume, dancing across the stage to her dramatic, exotic music. However, no one else in my elementary and junior high school was being taken to ballet lessons and orchestra concerts, and I actually got made fun of when I mentioned these things. Nevertheless, I loved dancing and was obsessed with Maria Tallchief, America's first prima ballerina and also the first Native American to hold that title, and of course I had a major crush on Rudolf Nureyev. I continued dancing when we moved to Philadelphia, taking lessons at the Pennsylvania School of Ballet. Though I eventually decided that I didn't want to seriously pursue it as a career, I continued taking classes off and on throughout my young adulthood. I've never stopped loving ballet and modern dance and, all types of social dancing.

When I was a kid I was fortunate to be taken on some exciting trips by my grandparents. My teacher-maternal grandmother took me along on a school trip with her fourth grade class to New York City when I was also in fourth grade. I remember going to the Empire State Building, and with my own money buying a little carved Madonna statuette in the gift shop of St. Patrick's Cathedral on the famous Fifth Avenue. In addition, my father's parents took my whole family to New York City for the 1964 World's Fair when I was 12. I felt very glamorous, staying in mid-town Manhattan at a fancy hotel, and going to see the Rockettes at Radio City Music Hall in Rockefeller Center, after which they showed the movie "Charade." At my age, I thought Cary Grant and Audrey Hepburn were the most sophisticated beings in the world. I'll also never forget the General Motors' Futurama displays of driverless cars and flying vehicles, the life-size automated talking Abraham Lincoln robot, and the "It's a Small World" ride at the World's Fair. That ride was subsequently moved to Disneyland. I know a lot of people now think it's the corniest, most insipid attraction, but I don't care; I loved it.

Another trip was even more fantastic (for a 17-year-old): my grandparents took us on a cross-country train trip from Philadelphia to the West Coast for the month of August 1969. We travelled through the South West, and my sister and I got to roam around on the train, often ending up in the glass observation car. The train made a short stop in Albuquerque and I remember seeing Native Americans for the first time in my life. We got off the train in Los Angeles, went to Disneyland,

and took a bus trip up the coast of California through Big Sur to San Francisco. After doing the sights there, we took another train trip through the mountains of Nevada, Utah, and Colorado, and eventually back home. My sister and I figured it was a plan to keep us from going to Woodstock, but we had the last laugh on our friends because instead we got to go to Haight-Ashbury.

Another factor that contributed to my love of the West is that in my 20s I was introduced to writings by and about Native Americans. I was sadly unaware of how many Native people had lived and still lived in the Northeast, and of how many had intermarried down through the generations with Black and white people, but I was intrigued by the spiritual writings and other books that were popular during that time. I read Hyemeyohsts Storm, a Northern Cheyenne's books, which relate things like the Medicine Wheel and the Sun Dance through traditional Native American teaching stories. I also read Ruth Beebe Hill's *Hanta Yo*, one of the first novels that I knew of to justly portray American Indians. Although *Hanta Yo* garnered a lot of negative criticism at the time, it nevertheless told a moving story of how a band of Sioux lived before the coming of the white man. These books and others led me to develop a sympathy for native people and to see them in a broader light than the way they had been portrayed in the television shows and movies I had seen as a child.

Chapter Three

Over the years of my marriage to Corny I had kept in touch with Shonna, one of the friends I had made in Livingston. In 1997, I was going through my divorce and decided it was time to go visit her and Montana. I planned to visit her at the end of August for a week and then go on for another week to see my sister, who lived in Oakland, California.

What I didn't know at first was that Shonna coincidentally had a single, divorced cousin she wanted to set me up with. The very first night I was there she introduced me to him and we went out as a foursome with her husband. Turned out he was the older brother of Shonna's cousin Kathy, whom I had met years before when visiting Montana. I vaguely remembered having heard about an older brother but didn't know anything about him. Tom was a college-educated accountant and he had quite a story about having campaigned for president in the run-up to the 1996 election. This was the year that Bob Dole won the Republican nomination for President. Though he withdrew from the race during the early primaries, Tom had written a book called *Balance the Budget: Now and How,* and apparently campaigned all over the country on this platform—which certainly impressed me with his courage and determination. He also had a rueful sense of humor about it. He said his claim to fame was that he even debated Lyndon LaRouche, Jr. in Idaho. At the end of that night, he invited me and Shonna and her 8-year-old son, Jake, to float the Yellowstone River with him the next day. We all had a ball together that day and I started feeling strongly attracted to Tom.

I had a great visit with Shonna, getting to know her husband and son and seeing other mutual friends, and of course I loved being in Montana. The sky, the dryness and lack of East Coast humidity, the sky, the mountains, the smell of sagebrush after a rain, The Sky. I had really missed all of that. There were times in New Jersey when we'd have a certain kind of weather in which the sky and particular kind of clouds would remind me of the skies in Montana. Not often, but once in a while we would have exceptionally clear and drier days with bright sun, and great big, tall, cumulus clouds and it would make me so homesick for the place.

A highlight of my stay was driving over the Beartooth Pass with Shonna and Jake. The road goes out of the East Entrance of Yellowstone Park, through a real "one-horse town" called Cooke City, and then climbs up to 10,947 feet. You truly feel like you've climbed up through the clouds to heaven. In the summer there is still snow along the side of the road, and you might even catch a glimpse of a mountain goat or two.

But mostly that week became about Tom. I developed quite a crush on him during the float trip, and like a school girl hoped that I would hear from him. Sure enough he called me and invited me out on a date. We spent the better part of a day together, going for a horseback ride, then a soak at Chico Hot Springs, and then dinner at their five-star restaurant. Our drive out of town that day was a little awkward since we didn't really know one another, so in an effort to make conversation I said that maybe he was unaware that I knew his sister Kathy. I related that in fact Kathy had loaned Corny and me her car when we had been out there for our honeymoon. There was a strange pause, then Tom said, "Was that the green Duster?" Not knowing how in the world he would know that, I said, "Y yes..." and he chuckled and said, "That's funny, I honeymooned in that car, too." It turns out that had been his father's car. He had loaned it to Tom, and later sold it to Kathy. We both kind of gulped at the uncanniness of this and the resultant feeling of predetermination.

By the end of the night I was crazy about him. Tom was smart and funny (unlike the stereotypical accountant), was exactly my age, and was, as the old saying goes, "a tall drink of water." I told him as he took me home to Shonna's house that I had plane reservations to go to the San

Francisco Bay Area for another week of vacation with my sister before I was returning to New Jersey. Coincidentally (Labor Day weekend was approaching), he told me he was flying there, too, for a visit with his daughter, who happened to live in San Francisco. Another synchronicity. This was years before the cell phone revolution so I gave him the phone number at my sister's, where I'd be staying, and he said he'd call me, that we should take advantage of the chance to see more of each other.

I arrived at my sister's not knowing whether I'd hear from him and was just tickled when my mother, who was also visiting, told me that there was someone named Tom on the phone for me. We managed to see each other multiple times while he was in the area, plus I met his daughter and he met my whole family. I learned that Tom had lived in Boulder, Colorado and in San Jose, California which meant that he had been exposed to life and culture outside of Montana. We talked about our political differences, namely that he was a Republican to my Democrat, and discussed some difficult things like our differing beliefs about abortion. He told me that, unlike many anti-abortion people, he was also opposed to the death penalty, which increased my respect for him. Overall he impressed me as being an honest, reasonable, and tolerant person. The last day we were together it was clear we wanted to pursue this and I joked with him about meeting halfway between Montana and New Jersey, for example in St. Louis for a weekend. And he amazed me by saying, "No way; I'll come to New Jersey." No one had ever gone that far out of their way for me before in my life. I was pretty much smitten at that point.

We carried on long distance for the next year, going back and forth between Montana and New Jersey, talking on the phone pretty much every night, and managing to see one another just about every month. In April Tom asked me to marry him and told me he would move to New Jersey if that's what I wanted, but that he'd prefer for me to move to Montana.

I had finished my psychologist's licensing exam the previous year, had just begun a fledgling private practice, and was working in a job that I didn't really like, which made moving seem reasonable. However, over my 20-year career I had worked in five different counties in New Jersey, had established expertise in the family violence/sexual abuse field, and had made many contacts—a crucial help in building a private practice, which was my purpose for getting my doctorate to begin with. This felt really hard to walk away from, not to mention leaving all my friends and family in the tri-state area. I also did a lot of soul-searching regarding the decision to marry Tom. Though I had not believed in love at first sight before meeting him, I now knew it existed and it felt really strong and right. At the same time, though, it felt crazy and impulsive to give up my whole life and move half-way across the country for a guy I hadn't yet known for a year (and a Republican?). But every time I went to Montana to see him, I just loved being there and being with him. He felt so much like "home," and so did Livingston. I also realized that this was different than some dating site match-up in that he came personally recommended by Shonna; I knew she wouldn't set me up with a guy who had a truck-load of problems. I almost could see the value in arranged marriages for the first time in my life.

Regarding giving up all of my professional contacts, I discovered that there was no other psychologist in full-time residence in Livingston. Tom also convinced me that the fact that he had an accounting practice and was a very active member of the social and business community would go far towards helping me build a practice. I also began to feel tired of the crush of people and traffic in my world (one of my last jobs had involved a three-hour round-trip commute), and the idea of living in a small town began to really appeal to me.

Where to get married was a bit of a dilemma. I didn't have any friends in the Lancaster area where my parents lived, my sister and her family lived in California, and most of my friends were in New Jersey. Meanwhile, pretty much all of Tom's friends and family were in the West. So we decided to find a place that would make us happy and figured if we didn't invite anybody, then nobody could be offended. We were going to be driving a U-Haul and towing my car across the country at the end of October, so we looked into which states en route didn't have a waiting period and settled on getting married in Rapid City, South Dakota. Getting married at Mount Rushmore didn't work out, though we did find a biker officiant if we had wanted him to marry us. We settled for the minister at a sweet little replica of a beautiful Norwegian stave church. By November 1, 1998, we were married and had moved me to Montana. Later we laughed about the fact that when we counted up the number of days we had actually been in one another's presence, it barely totaled 30 days.

Chapter Four

In Montana you tend to be more aware of the natural world around you—you can't ignore it as easily as in the East. The mountains and wild animals are all around you. You look up at the sky and the sky is HUGE and you can't as easily ignore the fact that you are on a ball hurtling through space. On a blue, clear day, as your eye travels upwards from the horizon, up, up, up, the sky actually changes color, getting darker and darker as you look straight up. This is because you are at a higher elevation and you're looking through far less humidity (and maybe pollution) than when you're standing on a street near sea level. At night, in most parts of the state, you can see millions, maybe thousands of millions of stars. The Milky Way isn't just some concept, it's a hard, concrete streak across the night sky and you realize how infinitesimally small we humans are. In a way, it's a little frightening, but I like being reminded of this.

On the other hand, in the megalopolis of the mid-Atlantic states, our urban lives and everything they involve seem to take on such urgency and importance. Urban civilization becomes the most important thing "in the world." Where you live and what you do for a living, how your car is running, who is mayor, what you're wearing tonight, whether you have a pimple, all seem more important to most people than the physical world around them. Children grow up not knowing that hamburger and eggs come from animals! Historically, city dwellers had trouble understanding why the government and weathermen couldn't control the weather better, although I think that's changing now with more people suffering with and becoming aware of climate change.

Yet, at the same time, in the city you have the ballet, and symphonies, and many and varied live music opportunities. There are magnificent art and science museums, libraries with ancient texts, and don't get me started on restaurants. Because of the huge numbers of people and their money, great halls of learning have been built, even if they are now being challenged to wake up and become more diversified.

The downside of life in Montana is mostly a result of the very thing that some people find appealing. It is the fourth-largest state by area, and according to the 2022 census, with approximately just seven people per square mile, it is one of the country's least densely populated states. Going anywhere out of Montana often requires traveling vast distances, so historically it has been quite expensive for people to leave. It has been only the wealthy who could afford to send their children out of state for college and arts training, and who could afford vacations to other parts of the country and world. This has led to a somewhat closed, provincial culture, with an ethos that if it can't be found in Montana, we don't need it. Of course not everyone exhibits this kind of thinking, but it's not unusual and it's one of the things I have found hard about living in Montana.

But just as Montanans evidence what I call a reverse-snobbism about urban culture, higher education, and Easterners, I have realized over my years of living in Montana that urban, coastal people have little idea who lives in what has been referred to as "fly-over country." This disrespectful phrase completely disregards the fact that the center of the country is basically America's breadbasket. For the most part, this is where wheat, barley, and other grains are grown, and where the bulk of cattle, sheep, and pigs are raised. We are friends with two couples who own working cattle ranches and I think very highly of them. The wife of one is the local district court judge! I'm reminded of the humorous *New Yorker* cover by Saul Steinberg from the 1970s that was turned into a popular poster. It depicts the view of the rest of the world westward from New York showing Manhattan as the center of the world in the foreground while the rest of the U.S., the Pacific, and Japan, China, and Russia vanish into the minuscule distance. This was meant as a caricature, but as a former

New Yorker and Northern Jersey resident, I know that its egocentrism isn't far off the mark.

What do I mean about finding it hard to live in Montana? First, in my professional life, with my doctorate and years of experience in the family violence and sexual abuse field, I naively thought that the social work/mental health community would welcome me and be interested in using my expertise for training, supervision, and leadership. With Tom's help, I had no problem quickly setting up a private therapy practice, but I was unprepared for how the culture had no idea what a doctorate was, or what psychotherapy was, and how behind the times the social work field was in terms of things like how to deal with incest cases. I won't bore the reader with professional protocol and standards details, but suffice to say it felt to me like going back 20 years. It was a bit of a rude awakening for me to also discover that everyone, no matter their degree, was called a "counselor." Many Montana readers might be thinking that I sound snobbish and condescending, but in the urban East Coast culture I come from, there was an understanding that doctoral psychologists had more intensive training than master's level people (usually about four or five years compared to two). We were therefore often sought out for clinical supervision, and pretty much without resentment were afforded the status of being addressed as "Dr." I know this sounds petty, and it's not like I really needed to be addressed that way, but it felt as though all my hard work to get through my doctoral training was being discounted. I also discovered that my years of additional training and work in the family violence field (for example, my past presentations at national and regional conferences) didn't garner much value. One year I excitedly called up one of my Department of Family Services colleagues to see if she or anyone was being sent to the next national conference on Adolescent Sex Offenders in Denver, since one can drive there in 10 hours. Disappointingly I found that no one was planning to go, and, not only that, but that the Department doesn't pay for out-of-state training.

It took me awhile to realize and understand what lay behind all of this. Because of the isolation and lower tax base, people in nearly every professional field have more or less had to chart their way with little or no outside guidance, and I grew to understand why there would be resentment towards out-of-staters with big degrees. In my experience in New Jersey, when an "expert" was coming from Boston or Virginia, we all wanted to go hear him or her talk. But I have grown to have more respect for what I call pioneer culture. In large part, Montanans are only about 100 years away from having been homesteaders. In 1900 you arrived with not much more than a few bags and trunks, and in order to make a life miles from civilization, out in the mountains or on the prairie, you had to do it by yourself, through your own ingenuity and grit. Ranches, farms, and homesteads were often 20 miles or more from any kind of town, and lest we forget, that's 20 miles by horseback. On the one hand, people here are known to loan you the shirt off their back if you need it. But on the other, they don't admit much to having intimate or emotional problems, much less talk about them, or ask for help. I think this comes from the learned stoicism that you either survived the losses of children and other tragedies or you "went under." And the numerous empty homesteads (called "ghost houses") out here, especially out on the prairie of eastern Montana, are a testament to how many people did go under.

One of the saddest things I had to face involved my work in the sexual abuse field. In New Jersey I had led therapy and self-help groups for adult sexual abuse survivors. This had been a very rewarding part of my professional career and I looked forward to continuing this in my private practice. Over a two-year period, I tried to start a number of groups, advertising in multiple newspapers and putting fliers up all over the community. I think I received a total of two calls. Of course part of the problem I faced was the fact that our entire county where I live has only about 15,000 people (as compared to millions in the Northern Jersey metropolitan area). However, if the accepted statistics are accurate, that approximately one woman in four has experienced some form of sexual abuse by the time she reaches age 18, there were probably enough women in Park County needing my support. But for whatever reasons they didn't or couldn't come forward. This was very hard for me to accept, both because I knew those women were out there, and because it meant something I loved doing in my work wasn't going to happen.

Don't get me wrong; I have loved living in Montana, loved living in a small town, where my office and basically everything I need to live are within 10 minutes of me. I remember in New Jersey having to spend more than half a day driving around in slow traffic just to do my Saturday errands. Obviously I don't miss the traffic in New Pensyl-Jersee-York, at all. I also love how when driving down a street in town I look at the other driver's faces because I'm likely to know them, unlike the anonymity of urban/suburban life. I love the folksy, funny Montana habit of the wave when you're out on a gravel ranch road and don't remotely know the other driver. There are whole conversations about what the proper etiquette is; do you lift your hand off the wheel or just lift a couple of fingers? I love how everything turns green in June while there is still snow up in the mountains. My dad used to say it was so green it practically hurt your eyes. I've loved hiking up in the mountains in high summer and afterwards either stopping at the Old Saloon in Emigrant for a beer or at the old-fashioned Pop Stand for ice cream. Though I can't do it anymore due to age-related injuries, I have loved riding horses up into the mountains and how they can get you up to higher altitudes without you having to do so much of the work. I love taking our 24-foot "cabin on wheels" up to mountain streams and lakes. I love sitting on the deck of my house and watching storms roll through, the view so immense that I can see three different weather events at once, including double rainbows. I love how when I was out riding my bike one day I nearly ran into a moose and her twin calves. I love taking company down to Yellowstone and seeing baby bison in the spring, hearing the elk bugling in the fall, stopping to see Old Faithful and the majestic Grand Canyon of the Yellowstone River, and hearing Tom make up crazy songs about "two million tourists who drive too slow." I love how the valley between Livingston and Yellowstone Park is actually called Paradise Valley. I love how my husband and I have made a goal of going to all the hot springs in Montana, which we have yet to complete. And yes, I love my quaint little western town of Livingston. For years, I would figuratively pinch myself when driving into the center of town, when I would see that big Northern Pacific Railroad Depot, and across the street, the neon sign of the Murray Hotel where the movie director Sam Peckinpah reportedly shot a bullet in the wall. I couldn't believe I was getting to live here!

However, I haven't loved the climate. Unlike the Mid-Atlantic states where there are four equal seasons, here in Montana we basically have six or seven months of winter, roughly four to six weeks each of spring and fall, and if we're lucky two, maybe two and a half months of summer. It's not that I mind winter; I love it when it snows. In fact, when I first moved here I enjoyed telling my friends back East how 20 degrees and dry snow was way better than 36 degrees and freezing rain. What's hard is the length of winter, some years it just goes on and on, and I really miss the East Coast spring. I wasn't aware of how much this would bother me when I first moved here, but it has grown more and more over the years. I suppose part of this is due to my aging. Let's face it, the outdoor winter activities that draw people to this area are not the greatest for many older folks (skiing, snowshoeing, climbing, etc.). I even fall too much cross-country skiing!

I also haven't mentioned the wind here in Livingston. The area called the Rocky Mountain Front, which runs south to north, is known for being very windy. We often have winds of 30-40 mph (natives, Tom included, call that "breezy"), and can have gusts to 60-80 mph in the winter. There is even a name for this effect, it's called the "kata-foehn" wind. One funny memory I have happened when I walked over to Tom's folks' house to visit his mom. It was a sunny, fall day of about 42 degrees, but the wind must have been blowing about 40 mph, because I couldn't believe it when she said, "Isn't this a nice day?" I think she meant it because it was sunny and above freezing, though I didn't think it was very lovely.

I have also found it hard socially. I'm a fairly gregarious person and before I moved to Montana I had never had trouble making friends anywhere I went. In Montana, however, it's been a challenge. In the 25 years I've been in Livingston, I'm sad to say, I've had and lost a number of friends because we just didn't have enough in common and couldn't relate to one another enough. Essentially because of the cultural differences, I get along best with women who either are from or have lived elsewhere. I even had an embarrassing experience in my early years in Livingston when I found out that a singing group I was part of didn't appreciate my opening my big fat East Coast mouth all the time and actually invited me to quit the group. My husband kids me about my New York interrupting-style of talking. I've tried to explain, I'm not really interrupting you, I'm talking WITH you. But I guess those gals in the group didn't think it was funny.

Speaking of my husband, one of my early shocks came at the first Easter or Thanksgiving dinner we went to at his parents' house. There were probably eight or so people at the table and I again embarrassed myself when I tried to strike up a conversation with the cousin sitting across from me, while others were talking down at the other end of the table. I didn't understand when they all stopped talking and looked at me that the rule was that one person spoke at a time. Heck, in the culture I come from, with its many Jewish, African-American, Italian, and Eastern European influences, people would be talking all at once all over one another! I'm reminded of a Garrison Keillor story from his "A Prairie Home Companion" show. He told a story about how the Norwegian/ Lutherans in Minnesota are such quiet people, they even do their religion quietly and don't appreciate when somebody "gets religion" and gets too loud about it in church. Truth is, quite a few Montanans are only one generation away from Minnesota, the Dakotas, and the other Midwestern states.

I did love Tom's folks. They were both from pioneer stock. His father was a first generation Swiss-American whose parents had attempted homesteading before moving to town to raise their family. I used to get so mad when he referred to graduate training as "college," but I noticed he stopped doing that when I was no longer the only family member with an advanced degree. (Bless you Emily and Jake!)

At the same time, I began to feel somewhat alienated from my urban friends. I have found as I have grown in my respect for and understanding of pioneer psychology, it has brought clearer to my mind how biased people on the coasts are, and how out of touch they are with what makes people in the interior of the country tick. In the beginning, when I first moved to Livingston, thinking like a psychologist, I thought learning about this cultural difference was interesting. But I found little interest among my friends, even among my former professional colleagues. I know I risk insulting those readers not from Montana, but that is what it has felt like to me.

In conclusion, this all has left me feeling both at home and alienated from both Montana and my home in the East.

Epilogue

I have begun to realize that the split between Montana and the East Coast is a representation of the differences between my mother and father. Yes my father became a lawyer and could be quite the intellectual, but for the most part, his heart was always in the country. My mother, on the other hand, was not outdoorsy and her heart was always more involved in city culture. Their personalities were also very different. My father was more of a laid-back, romantic who could be impractical at times, whereas my mother was a disciplined person who could be stern and demanding.

Let's face it, we're talking about being torn between two things and the feeling of ambivalence here. The truth is, if a person had to pick one word that has captured me in entirety, it would be ambivalence. I have had trouble in the past achieving things because of my ambivalence. If my analyst asked me 1000 times how I felt about something, 999 times I probably answered, "Well, I'm ambivalent...." I know now that it has to do with the conflicts I have had with both my parents, loving them and at the same time being very angry about things that went on in their marriage, in our home, and in my life. Yes I've painted a romantic picture of our life, but I've left out the painful reality that as a kid I felt that I had to choose between my parents, that I wasn't allowed to actually love both of them, and also that I felt like I couldn't really leave them and love someone else. This is why I could tolerate living in a bad marriage for as long as I did. It took me years of hard work and lots of pain to get to the point that I could emotionally separate from them, and it wasn't until I was nearly 50 that for the first time in my life there was something I DIDN'T feel ambivalent about: my handsome, loving husband, Tom.

One of the other things that over the years has begun to bother me about where I live is the whiteness; the lack of people of color. Yes, there are Indigenous, Native Americans who live in Montana. But considering how many "reservations" there are in the state, there are hardly any Indigenous people living in my area. This is particularly sad given that the geographic area where I live was once home to the Absaroka or Apsaalooke Crow people who were all forced to move to the Crow "reservation" about 195 miles from Livingston. I put the word reservation in quotes because the word stems from when Native peoples gave up large portions of their land through treaties; while some of it was supposed to be "reserved" for their use, as we know, it was often taken away from them or they were forcibly moved. The beautiful mountains outside of Livingston are called the Absaroka Mountains, named after these people. I find it so ironic and sad, that the white settlers gave American Indian names to things while at the same time not respecting and trying to obliterate the Native peoples.

As the years have gone by, Tom and I have grown more and more tired of the long winters up here in the North. We had gone to New Orleans in the spring years ago, for the New Orleans Jazz Fest. More recently, we went in February one year and March in another, both times for business trips, and discovered how lovely it can be there at that time of year. While still in deep winter here, it's full-on spring there! It can even get into the 80s in late March/April. I found quickly, too, that it reminded me of Philadelphia. Though the architecture was influenced more by the French and Spanish colonials than that in Philadelphia, the similarity is in the fact that much of the city was built in the 1700s and 1800s, as was Philadelphia. I love the fact that both cities have a lot of history to them. Of course it also reminds me of my years living in a culture more diverse than the one-note Caucasian majority culture of Montana. Not to mention the humidity in both places!

After numerous trips down to New Orleans, I have fallen in love with the place and find that I truly feel at home when I'm there. There is something about New Orleans that is completely unique and that has gotten under my skin. New Orleans ethnically and culturally is an amalgam of the English, French, Spanish, Caribbean, African, and Native American peoples who were the original settlers. There are even Cajun cowboys out in the country west of the city who wear cowboy hats! Most importantly, New Orleans is the city of music, and with my love of music, it just speaks to me. Tom and I can go out and hear professional music of practically any type, two or three times a week, sometimes even for free. And of course much of it is meant to be danced to.

New Orleans has become the perfect complement to my living in Montana. It doesn't really serve me to go back East in the winter, but the wild, colorful, creative character of New Orleans is like New York, Philly, and New Jersey all rolled up together, but in the tropics! They do say that New Orleans is the northern-most city in the Caribbean.

I've also found myself drawn to the Mardi Gras Indian tradition of New Orleans, which is a complex practice that weaves together parading, sewing complicated masquerading suits (don't call them costumes), and call and response songs or chants. It developed out of the fact that in the early days of New Orleans, enslaved people of color who escaped from their "masters" were often taken in by the native people (some of whom were also enslaved) and they also intermarried, thus many Black New Orleanians have Native American ancestors. The two peoples felt a resonance between their dancing and drumming, the intricate beadwork of their African and Native traditional clothing, and the shared legacy of resisting enslavement. I realize even as I write this that perhaps the reason I am drawn to this culture is because it represents a melding of the character of Montana with the East Coast, and of the differences between my father and mother.

There is something intangible in what New Orleans does for me. Maybe it's about connecting heart and mind.

Pictures

My mother and dad at the Elephant Head Ranch on Rte 20 near Cody, WY (1951)

Butte, MT circa 1910 (photo courtesy Butte-Silver Bow Public Archives)

My mom and I in front of our apartment complex in Butte circa 1953

(that's my Grandfather Jack in the back; I loved that suede jacket of hers,

and I even got to wear it in the late 60's!)

This is my grandparents, circa 1935, with some of their friends, the Michaud's

at their camp on Eagle Lake, Maine; Jack, laying down on the left,

and Ruth on the right in the rocker

Jack looking quite dapper with his Willis-Knight circa 1920s, probably in Boston while in Law School. I assume this is the car he drove across the country. I wonder if he and Ruth honeymooned in this car?

My dad, Mike, in his cowboy outfit circa 1940-41

probably before they went out West for the first time

My sister Bebe on the left with friends at the Israeli Folk Dances in Phila., circa 1969-1970

Mom, Bebe, Dad, and me in Rehoboth Beach, DE (1971)

One of the girls who worked in the kitchen at the 320 Ranch (1973)

My first attempt at a self-portrait - Bard College (1974 5)

Long Branch Saloon circa 1983, Livingston, MT (photo credit Corny Kocsis)

Me and Shonna in Paradise Valley, MT (1979-80)

Me and Bebe – New Year's Eve (1985)

VICTIMS' AID—Christine Hillegass, coordinator of Monmouth County's Sexual Abuse and Prevention Program, helps incest victims cope with that trauma.

Newspaper clipping about the work I was doing in 1986

Me enjoying a late afternoon at the Jersey Shore (1990)

My parents and Bebe and her kids at my house in Long Branch, NJ (1995)

The little Stav Kirke in Rapid City, S.D. where Tom and I were married (1998)

Tom and I in Yellowstone National Park (1999)

Wesley, a Mardi Gras Indian (2010, photo credit C. Hillegass)

Main Street, Livingston and the Absaroka Mountains (2023, photo credit C. Hillegass)

Acknowledgements

I would like to thank my longtime friend and colleague Paula Freed for her willingness to read my early manuscript and for her psychoanalytic feedback about this work. And thanks to my Montana friend, Jackie Art, for her helpful suggestions along the way and her editing of the final draft, and to Rob Park for helping with the design of my book cover. I also want to thank my writing coach and mentor Valerie Harms, without whom this book would not have been possible.

Finally, I want to thank my psychotherapist Dr. Barbara Gerson, for her patient guidance, insight, and encouragement through the years.

About the Author

Chris Hillegass has a master's degree in Forensic Psychology from the John Jay College of Criminal Justice, and a Psy.D. from Rutgers University. Chris received several awards for her work in New Jersey in the sexual abuse field in the 1980's, helping victims to overcome the societal shame and secrecy that unfortunately still plagues our world today. She worked in the mental health field for over 40 years before retiring from her private psychotherapy practice. Chris is also a talented photographer and has enjoyed capturing the magnificent Montana landscape and the life and culture of New Orleans. She and her husband, Tom Shellenberg, feel it is important to contribute to their Pennsylvania, Montana, and New Orleans communities, and enjoy travelling and spending time with Tom's daughter and her family. Chris and Tom reside most of the year in Livingston, Montana with their pit-bull mix, Cinnamon, who grew up on the Crow Indian Reservation and still doesn't understand the concept of fences.